MY TOURIST GUIDE TO
THE
DINOSAUR WORLD

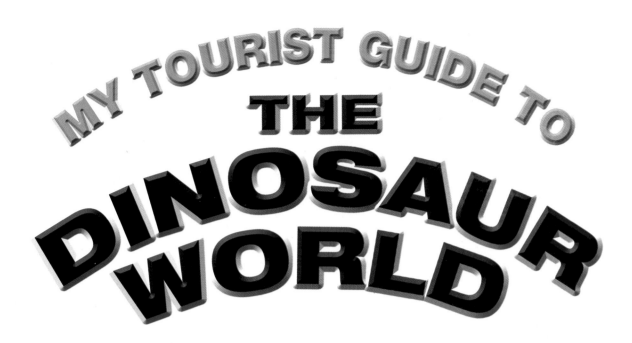

LONDON, NEW YORK, MELBOURNE,
MUNICH, AND DELHI

Written and edited by Sam Priddy

Senior art editor Smiljka Surla
Senior editor Ben Morgan
Designers Daniela Boraschi,
Alison Gardner, Peter Laws
Illustrators Katie Knutton, Maltings Partnership
Cartography Merritt Cartographic
Production editor Ben Marcus
Production controller Erika Pepe
Managing editor Julie Ferris
Managing art editor Owen Peyton Jones
Publisher Sarah Larter
Associate publishing director Liz Wheeler
Art director Phil Ormerod
Publishing director Jonathan Metcalf

Consultant Dr Darren Naish

First published in Great Britain in 2012 by
Dorling Kindersley Limited
80 Strand, London WC2R 0RL
A Penguin Company

Copyright © 2012 Dorling Kindersley Limited
2 4 6 8 10 9 7 5 3 1
001-184194–Jul/2012

A CIP catalogue record for this book
is available from the British Library

ISBN 978 1 4093 7630 9

Printed and bound in China by Hung Hing

Discover more at
www.dk.com

CONTENTS

PREPARING FOR YOUR TRIP

You're about to go on the ultimate prehistoric holiday: a trip into the past to see dinosaurs, mammoths, and Neanderthals. This will be a dangerous journey, but luckily your time machine is equipped with everything you'll need to make the most of your trip – and keep you alive.

Periscope
Just like in a submarine, a periscope is used to watch out for signs of danger.

Bedroom
Everyone sleeps in small bunk beds in the same room.

Bathroom
This room contains a toilet, a sink, and a shower.

Propellers
In case you need to venture underwater, propellers will power you through the oceans.

Engine room
Powerful engines are strong enough to drive the vehicle through any environment.

Garage
This room contains everything you need for exploring outside: an armoured vehicle, snowmobile, jetpacks, and a shark cage.

Ramp
In an emergency, the ramp can be lowered quickly to allow for a speedy getaway.

Tank treads
There are no roads in the prehistoric world, so tank treads are used to overcome difficult terrain.

Equipment room
Clothes and tools for all your prehistoric adventures can be found in this room.

Fireman's pole
If you ever need to get ready in a hurry, slide from the bedroom straight to the equipment room.

EARLY EARTH

FIRST ANIMALS

AGE OF FISH

AGE OF INSECTS

Communications dish
Radio signals help the tourists stay in touch with each other.

Solar panels
The Sun's energy can be harnessed to generate extra power for the time machine.

Time portal
To travel through time you'll drive through portals – gateways between different periods in the past.

Kitchen
You'll do your cooking in the kitchen. Essential food supplies are kept in a cupboard next door.

Intruder alarm
At the first sign of danger the intruder alarm will sound in the cockpit, alerting the drivers to the problem and locking down the vehicle.

First aid kit
Small wounds can be treated onboard, but for more serious problems you'll have to return to the modern world.

Cockpit
Everything is controlled from the cockpit, and information about the prehistoric world is available at the touch of a hand.

Headlights
Extremely bright lights are essential during the dark prehistoric nights.

Beamer
In order to travel forwards and backwards in time, the beamer creates a time portal.

Protective armour
The camper van is built to withstand batterings from charging dinosaurs.

Science lab
Throughout your holiday you can collect specimens and analyse them in the lab.

FIRST DINOSAURS

AGE OF GIANTS

END OF THE DINOSAURS

ICE AGE

AGE OF HUMANS

EARLY EARTH

At night the **Moon** is **very large** in the sky – it is **much closer** to the Earth during **this period** than in modern times.

THE PRECAMBRIAN PERIOD

▶ When: **4.6 billion to 550 million years ago**

The very early Earth is not a particularly nice place to visit. Scalding temperatures reach up to 80°C (176°F) and there's no oxygen – just a deadly atmosphere of nitrogen, methane, and carbon dioxide that's been belched up by volcanoes. You'll need to breathe air through a tank and wear a protective suit to survive the hellish conditions.

Asteroid
Chunks of space rock called asteroids hurtle into the Earth at great speed.

💬 TOURIST TIP

Earth attack

"*Smashing!*
We saw thousands of comets and asteroids crashing into the young planet. Apparently they're bringing water to Earth that will help to create the first oceans."

Activity: Comet spotting

YOU ARE HERE

EARLY EARTH

FIRST ANIMALS

AGE OF FISH

AGE OF INSECTS

VISIT A VOLCANO

There are lots of active volcanoes on the early Earth, and eruptions are common. It's worth climbing a volcano if you get the chance, but make sure you don't get too close to one that's about to explode.

DON'T MISS

Formation of the Moon

Early on in the Earth's history a Mars-sized planet will smash into it, creating a ring of dusty debris that will one day clump together to form our Moon. You'd have to be pretty brave to stick around for a photo though…

Life begins

Visit the late Precambrian to see signs of life on the shores of the first oceans. Dome-shaped rocky structures called stromatolites are built by communities of early forms of bacteria. They're producing oxygen that will be crucial for life to flourish in years to come.

WELCOME TO THE FIERY EARLY EARTH. THIS STAMP ENTITLES YOU TO STAY FOR AS LONG AS YOU CAN SURVIVE.

PRECAMBRIAN

Comet impact

The Earth's surface is torn apart by incoming comets (giant lumps of dirty space ice).

FIRST DINOSAURS

AGE OF GIANTS

END OF THE DINOSAURS

ICE AGE

AGE OF HUMANS

The ice **reflects heat** from the Sun **away** from Earth, making the planet **even colder.**

Frozen oceans ....
It's almost impossible to tell the difference between land and sea.

Thick ice ....
In places ice can be up to 1,000 m (3,300 ft) thick.

Head for the slopes!

There's not much to do on a frozen planet, so strap on some skis to make your way across the icy landscape.

"Literally the only fun thing to do here..."
The Prehistoric Journal

YOU ARE HERE

EARLY EARTH

FIRST ANIMALS

AGE OF FISH

AGE OF INSECTS

SKI ON A
SNOWBALL EARTH

Scientists aren't exactly sure why, but several times during Earth's history the entire planet has frozen over. For the ultimate winter vacation travel back 700 million years. Bitterly cold winds swirl around the icy planet and most forms of life have been killed off.

Chilly conditions
Average temperatures on the surface are around −50°C (−58°F). Brrr!

Icy equator
The ice reaches as far as the equator during a Snowball Earth period.

TOURIST TIP

Constant sunshine

"*A nice surprise.*
Although it was very cold when we went skiing, the Sun was always shining. All of the moisture was trapped under the ice so there were no clouds, meaning it never rained or snowed!"

★★★☆☆

Activity: Ski safari

VOLCANIC VENTS

To see any signs of life during this deep freeze you'll need to plunge beneath the ice to the bottom of the ocean, where you might find bacteria living near hot underwater vents. Be warned, though – chemicals from the vents have made the water toxic.

FIRST DINOSAURS   AGE OF GIANTS   END OF THE DINOSAURS   ICE AGE   AGE OF HUMANS

FIRST ANIMALS

THE CAMBRIAN PERIOD

▶ When: **542–488 million years ago**

The Cambrian Period may not seem like the most exciting time to visit – after all, 85 per cent of the planet is covered by oceans – but it's here that you'll see the first signs of life really blossoming on Earth. The ice of the Snowball Earth has melted away, and in its place a variety of new animals, such as worms and fish, are appearing in what's known as the Cambrian explosion.

THE CAMBRIAN TOURIST BOARD WELCOMES YOU TO A WATER WORLD FULL OF LIFE. PLEASE DON'T LITTER.

CAMBRIAN

Giant island
Throughout the Cambrian Period Laurentia moves southwards.

💬 TOURIST TIPS

Mind the claws

"Lethal...
We found an *Anomalocaris*, which looks a bit like a massive shrimp. It was using large claws attached to its head to catch prey."

★★★★☆

Attraction: Clawed creature

Bizarre creature

"Creepy!
When I first saw *Hallucigenia* I didn't know whether to scream or laugh. I couldn't even tell which part was its head!"

★★★★★

Attraction: Weird animal

Marvel at a Marrella

Go snorkelling to see a crazy-looking creature with 50 legs!

YOU ARE HERE

EARLY EARTH

FIRST ANIMALS

AGE OF FISH

AGE OF INSECTS

PANTHALASSIC OCEAN

AURENTIA

SIBERIA

APETUS OCEAN

BALTICA

GONDWANA

Animals start to **evolve jaws** in the Cambrian Period, and the world's **first predators** appear.

Water world
Cambrian Earth is a watery place. The Panthalassic and Iapetus oceans cover much of the planet.

Supercontinent
The giant continent of Gondwana begins to form at the end of the Cambrian.

WHERE TO GO

The land in the Cambrian Period is a lifeless place, with no animals or plants, just a barren landscape of damp and slimy rocks. But the oceans are full of strange and wonderful creatures to discover, so bring your diving equipment. Avoid the end of the period though, as temperatures reach an uncomfortable 55°C (131°F).

BEACHCOMBING

Explore the beaches in search of trilobites, prehistoric critters that look a bit like modern-day woodlice. They live in the ocean, scouring the seabed for food, but you might be able to find the shells of dead ones that have been washed ashore.

RST DINOSAURS

AGE OF GIANTS

END OF THE DINOSAURS

ICE AGE

AGE OF HUMANS

Although *Opabinia* looks fascinating, it's also very small. You'll need specialist diving equipment to see this amazing creature properly. Underwater digital cameras can be used to take detailed pictures of the critter, which can then be enlarged for closer study. Although you'll have to find the creature first...

NEED TO KNOW

Size:

Human thumb　　**Opabinia**

Location: Laurentia

Time: 515–500 million years ago

Diet: Soft, small items of food

What else to look out for:

Wiwaxia　　*Haikouichthys*

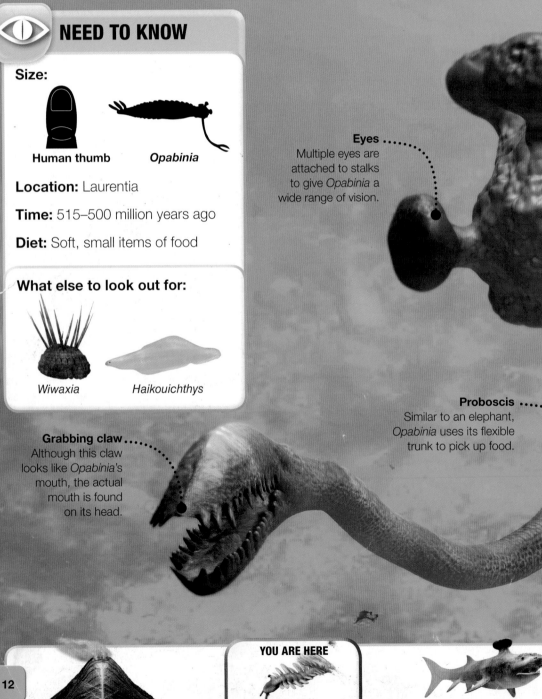

Segmented body .....
Opabinia's body is made up of 16 segments.

Eyes .....
Multiple eyes are attached to stalks to give *Opabinia* a wide range of vision.

Proboscis .....
Similar to an elephant, *Opabinia* uses its flexible trunk to pick up food.

Grabbing claw .....
Although this claw looks like *Opabinia*'s mouth, the actual mouth is found on its head.

EARLY EARTH　　**YOU ARE HERE** **FIRST ANIMALS**　　**AGE OF FISH**　　**AGE OF INSECT**

DISCOVER AN
OPABINIA

In a world full of bizarre creatures, *Opabinia* is probably the strangest. To catch a glimpse of one of these miniature monsters you'll need to head down to the bottom of the sea with a magnifying glass. Barely the size of a mouse, *Opabinia* has five eyes and a remarkable clawed trunk (called a proboscis), which it uses to pick up food from the seafloor, before gobbling it up in its mouth.

Side flaps
Opabinia swims using overlapping flaps on its sides.

Opabinia looks so **strange** that when it was presented to **scientists** in 1972 **everyone laughed.**

TOURIST TIP

Funky mover

"So weird...
I was interested to see how *Opabinia* moved. It moved flaps on its body up and down like a Mexican wave to propel itself through the water. Pretty cool!"

Activity: Ocean safari

IRST DINOSAURS   **AGE OF GIANTS**   **END OF THE DINOSAURS**   **ICE AGE**   **AGE OF HUMANS**

AGE OF FISH

New mountains
Two continents collided a
the start of the Devonian,
creating the Caledonian
Mountains in Euramerica.

THE DEVONIAN PERIOD

▶ When: **415–360 million years ago**

The Age of Fish certainly lives up to its name. Not only are the seas teeming with life, including the first ever sharks, but some pioneering fish are developing feet and making their way onto land. The Devonian Period is also a top tourist destination for plant lovers. The world's first forests are spreading inland from the coasts.

SIBERIA

PANTHALASSIC OCEAN

EURAMERICA

RHEIC OCEAN

Mountain climbing

Scale the newly formed Caledonian Mountains.

"The best views in all Euramerica!"
Devonian Climbing Weekly

EARLY EARTH

FIRST ANIMALS

YOU ARE HERE

AGE OF FISH

AGE OF INSECTS

WHERE TO GO

The Devonian is cooler than previous periods, but still warm enough for a nice summer holiday. Forests of *Archaeopteris* trees are common, and are a good spot to set up camp. Be wary of earthquakes as Euramerica and Gondwana move closer together.

FISH WITH LEGS

Euramerica is home to the strange-looking *Ichthyostega*, one of the first animals with four legs. Although it spends a lot of time in the water, *Ichthyostega* has developed limbs and is capable of pulling itself onto land. It also has lungs for breathing air.

Shallow seas
The seas around Euramerica are warm and shallow – perfect for scuba diving.

PLEASE TREAT OUR PLANET WITH CARE.

DEVONIAN IMMIGRATION AND CUSTOMS.

DEVONIAN

STAMP ALLOWS TRAVELLER TO STAY FOR 60 DAYS.

Warm oceans
Ocean temperatures get up to 30°C (86°F).

Lush forests
For the first time in Earth's history, forests cover much of the continent of Gondwana.

Keep your **eyes peeled** for a *Pterygotus*, a **giant sea scorpion** larger than a fully grown man.

GONDWANA

FIRST DINOSAURS

AGE OF GIANTS

END OF THE DINOSAURS

ICE AGE

AGE OF HUMANS

PREHISTORIC
SCUBA DIVING

The oceans around Euramerica are home to some truly terrifying fish. A scuba diving trip will bring you face-to-face with *Dunkleosteus*, an armoured monster that hunts in the shallow seas. Also keep an eye out for *Stethacanthus*, a shark with a strange structure on its back that looks like an ironing board.

Sharp fangs
Over time *Dunkleosteus*'s tooth plate wears down to leave sharp points.

NEED TO KNOW

Size:

Human   *Dunkleosteus*

Location: Euramerica

Time: 380 million years ago

Diet: Fish

Size:

Human   *Stethacanthus*

Location: Euramerica

Time: 380–350 million years ago

Diet: Fish

What else to look out for:

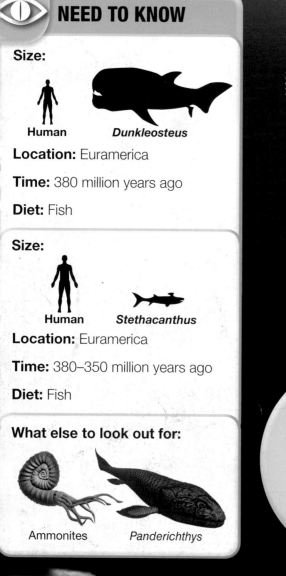

Ammonites   *Panderichthys*

Dunkleosteus's jaws are **so powerful** they can **crush concrete** with a single bite. Stay out of its way!

EARLY EARTH

FIRST ANIMALS

YOU ARE HERE

AGE OF FISH

AGE OF INSECTS

Ironing board
Stethacanthus's strange dorsal fin is covered in small spikes. Its use is a mystery.

Bony armour
Dunkleosteus has plates of bone up to 5 cm (2 in) thick to protect it from even bigger predators.

Like their modern cousins, prehistoric sharks shed teeth throughout their life. If you look closely you may be able to find some souvenirs at the bottom of the ocean.

Teeth of the shark *Cladoselache*

RST DINOSAURS   AGE OF GIANTS   END OF THE DINOSAURS   ICE AGE   AGE OF HUMANS

AGE OF INSECTS

THE CARBONIFEROUS PERIOD

▶ When: **360–300 million years ago**

You'll notice that everything is changing in the Carboniferous Period. Continents move closer together and eventually collide, while forests continue to spread. Insects are absolutely everywhere, providing food for the four-legged animals that are making the land their home as they say goodbye to life in the seas for good.

Smelly swamps ....
Tropical swamps cover much of Euramerica.

PANTHALASSIC OCEAN

🌴 WHERE TO GO

Swamp forests dominate the wet Early Carboniferous. Their remains will form the huge coal deposits that we'll use to heat our homes in the future. Giant trees such as *Lepidodendron* dominate the land, growing 40 m (130 ft) tall. Pack rubber boots and insect spray.

Large forests mean a greater chance of **forest fires.** Be careful when lighting your **campfire.**

CARBONIFEROUS TOURIST BOARD IMMIGRATION
ENTITLES HOLDER TO STAY FOR THREE MONTHS.
CARBONIFEROUS
WE ARE NOT RESPONSIBLE FOR YOUR INSECT BITES.

Collision ....
Gondwana and Euramerica collide to become a single giant continent.

EARLY EARTH

AGE OF INVERTEBRATES

AGE OF FISH

YOU ARE HERE

AGE OF INSECTS

SIBERIA

EURAMERICA

TOURIST TIP

Snake imposter

"How strange...
I thought snakes didn't appear until the Cretaceous, so I was surprised to see this slippery character. It turns out that Phlegethontia isn't a real snake, but a legless amphibian."

★★★☆☆

Attraction: Awesome amphibian

Giant millipede

"Scary!
I was wandering though the forests of Euramerica when I was startled by a huge millipede. *Arthropleura* grows to 2 m (7 ft) in length – I ran away screaming!"

★★★★☆

Attraction: Giant bug

PALEO-TETHYS OCEAN

Chilly World

Grab your snowboard! Ice sheets cover the southern tip of the planet – perfect for extreme sports.

GONDWANA

•••••••••••••••• South Pole
An ice cap covers part of Gondwana.

FIRST DINOSAURS

AGE OF GIANTS

END OF THE DINOSAURS

ICE AGE

AGE OF HUMANS

HUNT A GIANT
DRAGONFLY

As you arrive in the Late Carboniferous you'll notice that many of the insects buzzing through the forests are gigantic. Scientists aren't sure why this is, but think it might be because Earth's air is richer in oxygen during this period. Grab a large insect net and try and catch a *Meganeura*, a huge critter that may be the largest insect that has ever lived.

Wings ...
Meganeura flaps its front and back wings separately for maximum flight control.

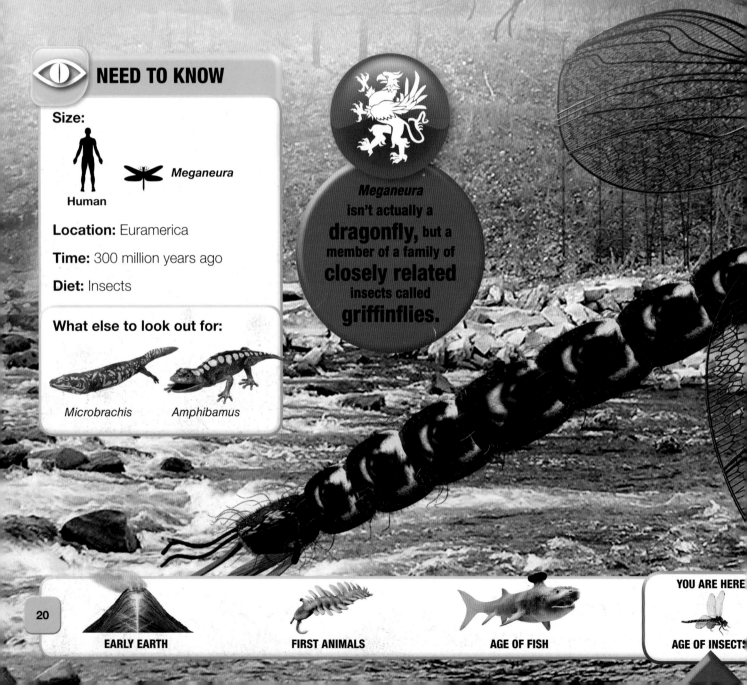

NEED TO KNOW

Size:

Human   *Meganeura*

Location: Euramerica

Time: 300 million years ago

Diet: Insects

What else to look out for:

Microbrachis   *Amphibamus*

Meganeura isn't actually a **dragonfly,** but a member of a family of **closely related** insects called **griffinflies.**

EARLY EARTH   FIRST ANIMALS   AGE OF FISH   YOU ARE HERE

AGE OF INSECTS

TOURIST TIP

On the hunt

"Lethal killer!
We saw a pair of *Meganeura* hunting.
They used their huge eyes to spot
prey, which they grabbed in mid-flight
before shoving it into their mouths.
All while they were still in the air!"

⭐⭐⭐☆☆

Activity: Hunting trip

Meganeura has a
wingspan
that's **12 times**
greater than that
of modern-day
dragonflies.

WHERE TO GO

The Triassic is one of the warmest periods in Earth's history. Because Pangaea is so large, the areas furthest from the sea have turned into hot, dry deserts, while the coastal areas are greener. Beware of rainy seasons near the equator.

Pole to pole
The continent of Pangaea stretches all the way from the North Pole to the South Pole.

DUNE BUGGYING

The ultimate desert activity – fast enough to escape most dinosaurs!

Dinosaurs don't yet rule the world. The top Triassic predators are a group of **archosaurs** related to modern **crocodiles.**

PANGAEA

Hot and dry
The interior of Pangaea is a vast, hot desert where few animals can survive.

EARLY EARTH

FIRST ANIMALS

AGE OF FISH

AGE OF INSECTS

FIRST DINOSAURS

THE TRIASSIC PERIOD

▶ **When: 251–200 million years ago**

Welcome to Pangaea – the single, giant continent that dominates Earth in the Triassic. Here you'll find all sorts of new and interesting creatures, from small mammals and frogs to the first dinosaurs. These animals evolved after a mysterious catastrophe wiped out 90 per cent of Earth's species at the start of the Triassic.

ALEO-TETHYS OCEAN

TETHYS OCEAN

Island life
The best places to see wildlife are islands and coastlines, where conifer forests teem with strange reptiles.

TRIASSIC TOURISM AND IMMIGRATION. THIS STAMP ENTITLES YOU TO STAY IN THE TRIASSIC FOR 30 DAYS.

TRIASSIC

TOURIST TIP

Dinosaur killer

"Run for your life!
The scariest creature I saw in the Triassic was *Postosuchus*, a large reptile at the top of the food chain. I saw it gnawing on the bones of a small dinosaur."

⭐⭐⭐⭐⭐

Attraction: Desert trek

THE FIRST DINOSAURS

Coelophysis is small and speedy, like several of the dinosaurs you can see in the Triassic. You'll need to be quick with your camera to get a good shot of these meat eaters as they scamper through the undergrowth.

YOU ARE HERE

FIRST DINOSAURS

AGE OF GIANTS

END OF THE DINOSAURS

ICE AGE

AGE OF HUMANS

Size:

Nothosaurus

Human

Location: Northeast Pangaea

Time: 240–210 million years ago

Diet: Fish

What else to look out for:

Odontochelys *Diphydontosaurus*

Metoposaurus *Lariosaurus*

Fish food ....
Triassic oceans are full
of fish and squid for
Nothosaurus to eat.

GO FISHING WITH
NOTHOSAURUS

While you're visiting the Triassic Period why not go fishing with
a true expert? *Nothosaurus* is a marine reptile that comes up
onto land to breathe and rest, much like modern-day seals,
but in the water it's an awesome killer. Try to keep up as it
uses its powerful tail to chase its prey, but watch out when
it grabs the fish with its long, sharp teeth.

EARLY EARTH

FIRST ANIMALS

AGE OF FISH

AGE OF INSECTS

Sharp teeth
Startled prey are
trapped inside a cage
of interlocking teeth.

Muscular neck
Nothosaurus twists
its strong neck sharply
to catch passing fish.

Nothosaurus
swims like an **otter**,
waving its long and
muscular tail
to power itself
forward.

SUNBATHING

For the best photos, find a
Nothosaurus on land – they're
too fast underwater to get
a good shot. It's a clumsy
creature out of the sea, and
without its clawed feet it would
have trouble moving about at all.

Paddle feet ....
Nothosaurus uses its
webbed feet for twisting
and turning underwater.

YOU ARE HERE

RST DINOSAURS

AGE OF GIANTS

END OF THE DINOSAURS

ICE AGE

AGE OF HUMANS

25

NEED TO KNOW

Size:

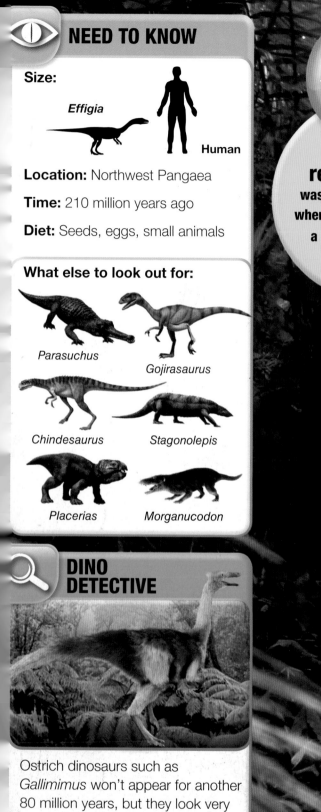

Effigia

Human

Location: Northwest Pangaea

Time: 210 million years ago

Diet: Seeds, eggs, small animals

What else to look out for:

Parasuchus

Gojirasaurus

Chindesaurus

Stagonolepis

Placerias

Morganucodon

DINO DETECTIVE

Ostrich dinosaurs such as *Gallimimus* won't appear for another 80 million years, but they look very similar to *Effigia*. If you investigate you'll discover it's a result of having the same sort of lifestyle.

Scientists first **realised** *Effigia* wasn't a **dinosaur** when they noticed it had a **crocodilian ankle.**

Toothless beak
Without teeth *Effigia* relies on its beak to crack open seeds.

EARLY EARTH

FIRST ANIMALS

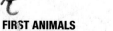

AGE OF FISH

AGE OF INSECTS

EXPLORE WITH
EFFIGIA

Dinosaurs aren't common in the Late Triassic period, but you might be forgiven for thinking they are if you come across an *Effigia*. Running on its hind legs, with small arms and a long tail, it looks and moves like a dinosaur, but is in fact a reptile in the same family as crocodiles. Follow it through the rainforest to see if it behaves like a dinosaur too.

Small arms
Effigia doesn't use its arms much, picking up food with its beak instead.

Stiff tail
Effigia's long tail is held up for balance.

YOU ARE HERE

FIRST DINOSAURS

AGE OF GIANTS

END OF THE DINOSAURS

ICE AGE

AGE OF HUMANS

27

AGE OF GIANTS

THE JURASSIC PERIOD

▶ When: **200–145 million years ago**

Welcome to the Jurassic, one of the most amazing periods in Earth's history. Following a mass extinction at the end of the Triassic that killed most of their competitors for food, dinosaurs are now thriving – and growing to enormous sizes. Graceful, long-necked giants called sauropods graze among the treetops, while bloodthirsty killers such as *Allosaurus* stalk the land in search of meat.

Northern lands ⋯⋯⋯⋯⋯
Earth's northern continent is breaking up to form North America, Europe, and Asia.

NORTH AMERICA

WHERE TO GO

The Jurassic is the perfect period for jungle explorers and beach lovers. It's warm and humid, and lush rainforests cover much of the land. The giant continent that existed in the Triassic has broken up, creating long coastlines where the jungle meets sandy beaches, turquoise lagoons, and coral reefs.

Sauropod Safari

Including *Brachiosaurus* there are 25 different sauropod species in North America – see if you can spot them all!

SOUTH AMERICA

Southern continent ⋯
The great continent of Gondwana stretches from the equator to the South Pole.

EARLY EARTH

FIRST ANIMALS

AGE OF FISH

AGE OF INSECTS

No ice
The poles are free of ice in the Jurassic because of the warm climate.

LAURASIA

EUROPE

TOURIST TIP

Archaeopteryx

"Is it a bird?
We were surprised to see a small, feathered creature flying between the trees. Called *Archaeopteryx*, it's said to be the world's first bird, but it looked more like a feathered dinosaur to me."

Activity: Bird watching

Tropical seas
Shallow tropical seas cover the area that will later become western Europe.

TETHYS OCEAN

Toxic gas from erupting volcanoes caused a **mass extinction** at the start of the Jurassic period.

GONDWANA

AFRICA

ANTARCTICA

JURASSIC TOURIST BOARD GRANTS THE BEARER PERMISSION TO VISIT THE JURASSIC FOR 30 DAYS.

JURASSIC

PLEASE ENSURE YOU TAKE ALL NECESSARY SAFETY PRECAUTIONS.

FIRST DINOSAURS

YOU ARE HERE

AGE OF GIANTS

END OF THE DINOSAURS

ICE AGE

AGE OF HUMANS

STEGOSAUR SALAD

If you carefully approach a *Kentrosaurus* from the front you may be able to get close enough to feed it without scaring it away. They feed on low-lying plants, so bring along ferns, mosses, seeds, or fruits to give them a tasty snack.

Moss

Ginkgo berries

Fern

NEED TO KNOW

Size:

Kentrosaurus   **Human**

Location: Gondwana

Time: 156–150 million years ago

Diet: Ferns, mosses, and berries

What else to look out for:

Giraffatitan   Dicraeosaurus

Shoulder spikes are common in stegosaurs – they're used to **fend off** unwelcome meat-eating dinosaurs.

EARLY EARTH   **FIRST ANIMALS**   **AGE OF FISH**   **AGE OF INSECTS**

PICNIC WITH A
KENTROSAURUS

A member of the stegosaur family, *Kentrosaurus* is smaller than its famous cousin *Stegosaurus* and has a couple of impressive shoulder spikes. It's best to sneak up on *Kentrosaurus* without it noticing you. This stupid creature has a brain the size of a walnut and may take a swing at you with its spiked tail if it mistakes you for a hungry predator.

DINO DETECTIVE

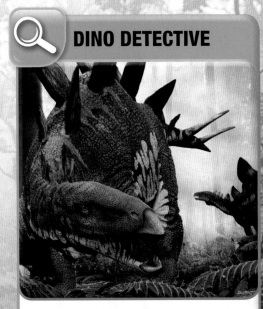

Travel to Jurassic North America to find a *Stegosaurus* and try to figure out what its back plates are for. They're probably not for defence – it's more likely they're used to control body temperature or are simply for display purposes.

FIRST DINOSAURS

YOU ARE HERE

AGE OF GIANTS

END OF THE DINOSAURS

ICE AGE

AGE OF HUMANS

31

Row of spines
Pointed spines run all the way along *Barosaurus*'s body. They may be used for display or defence.

Tough skin
Scaly skin helps protect these giants from the teeth and claws of hungry carnivores.

NEED TO KNOW

Size:

Barosaurus

Human

Location: North America

Time: 155–145 million years ago

Diet: Leaves

What else to look out for:

Camptosaurus

Diplodocus

Gargoyleosaurus

Camarasaurus

Dryosaurus

Othnielosaurus

Zip line!
Attach a rope-slide to two trees and swing between the dinosaurs as they feed.

EARLY EARTH

FIRST ANIMALS

AGE OF FISH

AGE OF INSECTS

TREE-TOP TOUR WITH
BAROSAURUS

With a giant, bulky body as long as a school bus, *Barosaurus* is one of the largest land animals that has ever lived. For the best views of a herd, climb up into the trees to see them browsing for food. They use their 9.5-m (30-ft) long necks to reach the top leaves.

Barosaurus's huge neck is a whopping five times longer than that of a giraffe.

Tiny head
Like most members of the large, plant-eating dinosaurs that make up the sauropod family, *Barosaurus* has a small head and brain.

RST DINOSAURS

YOU ARE HERE
AGE OF GIANTS

END OF THE DINOSAURS

ICE AGE

AGE OF HUMANS

33

Outstretched tail

When running at speed *Allosaurus* keeps its tail held up for balance.

Size:

Allosaurus

Human

Location: North America

Time: 150 million years ago

Diet: Meat

What else to look out for:

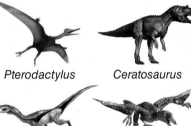

Pterodactylus

Ceratosaurus

Compsognathus

Archaeopteryx

Stegosaurus

Powerful legs

Strong hind legs help *Allosaurus* to reach great speeds when chasing prey.

STAR SCAVENGER

As well as hunting prey, it's common to find an *Allosaurus* feeding on the carcass of a dead dinosaur it's just happened to come across. They particularly like giant plant-eating sauropods such as *Brachiosaurus*, which can provide enough meat to feed them for several days.

EARLY EARTH

FIRST ANIMALS

AGE OF FISH

AGE OF INSECT

Horns
Horns on the male's head are used to impress females.

Slicing teeth
Allosaurus's teeth are capable of ripping through flesh like a saw.

Sharp claws
Long, deadly claws are used to hook into prey and tear them apart.

Allosaurus is a **cannibal** and will eat **members** of its own **species** if they get in its way at a **feeding site.**

RACE AN
ALLOSAURUS

Bearing a striking similarity to *T. rex* (who won't appear for another 70 million years), the flesh-eating predator *Allosaurus* is one of the Jurassic's top attractions. Although adults rely on ambushing prey, youngsters are much faster, using their powerful hind legs to run down victims. Race alongside a juvenile *Allosaurus* to find out exactly how fast they are.

FIRST DINOSAURS

YOU ARE HERE

AGE OF GIANTS

END OF THE DINOSAURS

ICE AGE

AGE OF HUMANS

CRETACEOUS TOURIST BOARD RESIDENT PERMIT.

CRETACEOUS

VALID FOR ONE YEAR – IF YOU SURVIVE THAT LONG!

Inland sea
The Western Interior Seaway runs across North America.

NORTH AMERICA

TETHYS OCEAN

NORTH ATLANTIC OCEAN

AFRICA

SOUTH AMERICA

Impact zone
The deadly asteroid will hit Mexico.

Jet skiing

If you're a fan of water sports, the Cretaceous is for you. Warm shallow seas cover much of Europe and North America – but watch out for sea monsters.

TOURIST TIP

Feathered dinosaurs

"So confusing!
We saw birds that looked like mini dinosaurs and feathered dinosaurs that looked like giant flightless birds! I didn't realize how closely related dinosaurs and birds were."

★★★☆☆

Attraction: Dinobird watching

Continental drift
Once joined together, South America and Africa are now moving apart.

EARLY EARTH

FIRST ANIMALS

AGE OF FISH

AGE OF INSECTS

END OF THE DINOSAURS

THE CRETACEOUS PERIOD

▶ **When: 145–65 million years ago**

The Cretaceous is the last of the three major periods in which dinosaurs roam the Earth. A top choice for time travellers, this period is home to the most famous and ferocious dinosaurs of all. The continents have drifted farther apart since the Jurassic and are starting to take their modern shapes. The weather is mostly warm, but watch out for cold spells when Australia freezes over.

Heading north
Africa is drifting north towards Europe, which is mostly underwater.

The asteroid that spells the end of the dinosaurs is due to hit **Mexico** at the very end of the Cretaceous. **Watch from a safe distance!**

FLYING KILLER

Don't miss the chance to get some shots of *Quetzalcoatlus*, the largest flying animal of all time. The size of a fully grown giraffe, it's amazing to watch as it unfolds its vast wings and takes to the air. It can be seen in Late Cretaceous North America soaring high overhead on the lookout for prey.

WHERE TO GO

Visit the forests of North America to see the legendary dinosaurs *Tyrannosaurus* and *Triceratops*. In the deserts of China you'll find *Velociraptor* and other bird-like, feathered dinosaurs. Come in the Late Cretaceous if you like gardening. Flowering plants such as magnolias (above) have made their first appearance on Earth, and you'll see them everywhere.

FIRST DINOSAURS **AGE OF GIANTS** **YOU ARE HERE**   **END OF THE DINOSAURS** **ICE AGE** **AGE OF HUMANS**

GO ON SAFARI WITH
SAUROPELTA

Unlike some armoured dinosaurs, *Sauropelta* doesn't have a club at the end of its tail, so it relies instead on huge neck spines and armour plates to protect it from attack. It's fun to take a safari ride with a herd of these heavyweights as they lumber along. You'll need a good driver, as well as an armoured car to withstand the occasional bash from the dinosaurs' tails.

Sauropelta's **tail** makes up almost **half** its **body length.** It contains more than **40 bones.**

Neck spines ....
Huge spines of bone protect *Sauropelta's* neck and throat from attack by predators.

NEED TO KNOW

Size:

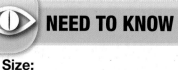

Sauropelta

Human

Location: North America

Time: 129–99 million years ago

Diet: Low-growing plants

What else to look out for:

Gastonia   Tenontosaurus

Stocky legs ..
Weighed down by its heavy armour, *Sauropelta* walks slowly on all fours, but it is also capable of sudden bursts of speed.

EARLY EARTH

FIRST ANIMALS

AGE OF FISH

AGE OF INSECTS

Back studs ....
Large studs of bone, surrounded by a mosaic of smaller studs, form a tough but flexible shield covering *Sauropelta*'s back and tail.

Armoured car
Drive slowly and carefully in the herd. Sudden movements or loud noises could make the animals panic and attack the car.

WANTED
DEAD OR ALIVE

REWARD
Packs of the fast and intelligent hunter **Deinonychus** have been known to attack *Sauropelta*. Keep an eye out for this **feathered predator.**

Beak
Sauropelta uses a narrow beak to pick out leaves one at a time when it's feeding.

NEED TO KNOW

Size:

Ornithocheirus

Human

Location: Europe, South America

Time: 110 million years ago

Diet: Fish

What else to look out for:

Aucasaurus

Irritator

TOURIST TIP

Fast flyer

"Absolutely incredible! We followed *Ornithocheirus* from South America to Africa and the pterosaur barely flapped its wings! No wonder it's found all over the world.*"*

⭐⭐⭐⭐⭐

Activity: Flying trip

Go fishing with a pterosaur!

Ornithocheirus is an expert fisher – together you could catch a big haul!

Teeth
Sharp teeth lining the jaws are perfect for catching fish.

EARLY EARTH

FIRST ANIMALS

AGE OF FISH

AGE OF INSECTS

Thin snout
Ornithocheirus has a bony crest at the end of its snout.

GLIDE WITH A
PTEROSAUR

Soar through the skies alongside *Ornithocheirus*, a giant pterosaur the size of a small aeroplane. Although it's one of the largest flying animals to ever live, its hollow bones and slender build make it ideal for flying. A journey over the Cretaceous landscape with one of these reptiles is not to be missed.

Eyes
Keen eyesight helps pterosaurs spot prey in the oceans.

Wings
Ornithocheirus's wingspan can be up to 6 m (20 ft) long.

Ornithocheirus means **"bird hand"**. However, pterosaurs are **not closely related** to birds.

IRST DINOSAURS

AGE OF GIANTS

YOU ARE HERE

END OF THE DINOSAURS

AGE OF MAMMALS

AGE OF HUMANS

NEED TO KNOW

Size:

Human   *Elasmosaurus*

Location: Western Interior Seaway

Time: 99–65 million years ago

Diet: Fish, squid, and shellfish

What else to look out for:

Mosasaurus

Ammonites

Protostega

Elasmosaurus has such a **long neck** that when its bones were first found, people thought the **neck** was the **tail**, and stuck its head on the **wrong end.**

Tiny head
Elasmosaurus has a small head and comes to the surface to breathe air.

Long neck
Elasmosaurus's neck contains an amazing 71 bones. (Giraffes only have seven neck bones!)

SWIM WITH
ELASMOSAURUS

Dive down into the Western Interior Seaway in North America to see an *Elasmosaurus*, a giant plesiosaur that cruises the ocean. The first thing you'll notice is its enormous neck. It stretches for more than half of its total body length and is so heavy that *Elasmosaurus* has difficulty lifting it out of the water.

EARLY EARTH

FIRST ANIMALS

AGE OF FISH

AGE OF INSECTS

Bulky body
Elasmosaurus is a
heavy creature and
swims slowly through
the ocean stalking
shoals of fish.

TOURIST TIP

Attack from below

"Don't get too close!
I thought this was a gentle giant
until I saw its huge teeth. It lay in
wait on the sea floor, and then its
neck darted upwards to snatch
fish. It was quite scary."

⭐⭐⭐☆☆

Activity: Deep-sea diving

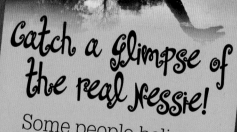

LOCH NESS
Sightseeing Tours

*Catch a glimpse of
the real Nessie!*

Some people believe
the Loch Ness Monster
is an *Elasmosaurus*.

IRST DINOSAURS

AGE OF GIANTS

YOU ARE HERE

END OF THE DINOSAURS

ICE AGE

AGE OF HUMANS

43

NEED TO KNOW

Size:

Corythosaurus

Human

Location: North America

Time: 76–74 million years ago

Diet: Ferns, fruits, and leaves

What else to look out for:

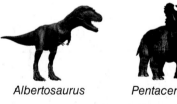

Albertosaurus

Pentaceratops

Euoplocephalus

Backbone
A tall ridge runs along the back, perhaps to make the dinosaur look larger.

LIVING IN HERDS

Some plant-eating dinosaurs rely on armour, weapons, or speed to protect themselves from predators, but duck-billed dinosaurs rely on safety in numbers. In a herd there are dozens of eyes and ears on the lookout all the time, making it hard for predators to sneak up on them.

EARLY EARTH

FIRST ANIMALS

AGE OF FISH

AGE OF INSECTS

Meaning "helmet lizard", *Corythosaurus* is named after the **helmets** worn by Corinthian soldiers in Ancient Greece.

Duck-like beak
Corythosaurus uses its beak to pluck leaves and twigs off trees.

Colourful crest
As well as making sounds, crests are brightly coloured to impress potential mates.

HEAR A DUCK-BILLED
CORYTHOSAURUS

As you make your way through the forests and swamps in North America, you might hear the unique sounds of a *Corythosaurus*. Hollow crests on the heads of these plant eaters are used as trumpets to make loud, booming calls. Like other duck-billed dinosaurs, *Corythosaurus* makes honking noises to keep in touch with the herd and warn others of danger.

FIRST DINOSAURS

AGE OF GIANTS

YOU ARE HERE

END OF THE DINOSAURS

ICE AGE

AGE OF HUMANS

Size:

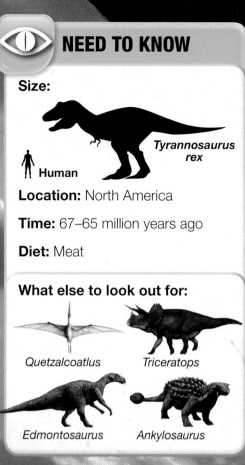

Human

Tyrannosaurus rex

Location: North America

Time: 67–65 million years ago

Diet: Meat

What else to look out for:

Quetzalcoatlus

Triceratops

Edmontosaurus

Ankylosaurus

FLUFFY BABIES

Although their parents have scaly skin, *T. rex* babies have a few fluffy feathers to keep them warm while they're growing up. Try to get close enough to one to take a photo, but keep an eye out for its mum.

Long tail
T. rex maintains balance even when running at speed, by holding out its stiff tail.

HUNT WITH A
TYRANNOSAURUS

Tyrannosaurus rex is the most famous dinosaur of all time, and the top predator in the Cretaceous. Follow from a safe distance as it hunts a *Triceratops*. It kills its victim quickly with a colossal bite that easily crunches through flesh and bone. The dead dinosaur is then ripped apart as *T. rex* feasts on its bloody remains.

T. rex is the **undisputed ruler** of Cretaceous North America. Its name means **"king of the tyrant lizards".**

EARLY EARTH

FIRST ANIMALS

AGE OF FISH

AGE OF INSECTS

Incredible eyesight ....
Excellent vision helps
T. rex to target prey
from great distances.

Sharp teeth ....
T. rex has up to
58 razor sharp teeth in its
mouth. Many are capable
of piercing bone.

Tiny arms
T. rex's forearms are
too small to be useful
when hunting. Its
hands only have
two fingers each.

Powerful legs .....
Large, athletic legs are
used to stamp on prey
to hold it still.

Visit *T. rex*'s Asian cousin Tarbosaurus

This fearsome dinosaur
has more teeth than
Tyrannosaurus rex!
Find it roaming the
plains of the Far East.

RST DINOSAURS

AGE OF GIANTS

YOU ARE HERE

END OF THE DINOSAURS

ICE AGE

AGE OF HUMANS

47

SEE A STAMPEDE OF
TRICERATOPS

One of the most impressive sights in the Late Cretaceous is a herd of stampeding *Triceratops*. But don't get in the way of a group of adults that have been spooked by the sight of a predator. *Triceratops* are the size of elephants and you'd be flattened to a pancake in a second.

Triceratops means **"three-horned face"**. The horns can grow to **1.2 m (4 ft)** in **length.**

NEED TO KNOW

Size:

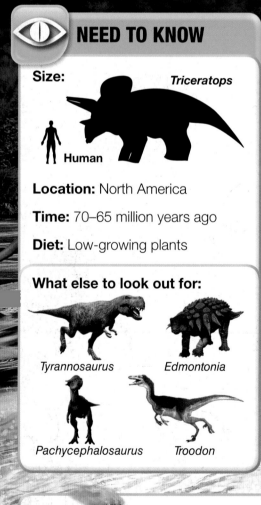

Triceratops

Human

Location: North America

Time: 70–65 million years ago

Diet: Low-growing plants

What else to look out for:

Tyrannosaurus

Edmontonia

Pachycephalosaurus

Troodon

Horny beak
A powerful bill is used to grasp and tear thick vegetation.

Giant head
Triceratops holds its heavy head close to the ground. It can only feed on low-growing plants.

EARLY EARTH

FIRST ANIMALS

AGE OF FISH

AGE OF INSECTS

Neck frill
Made of bone, the frill is
used to impress females
during the mating season.

Horns
Long brow horns just
bove the eyes are used
o scare away enemies.

MORTAL ENEMIES

Triceratops skulls have been found
with *Tyrannosaurus* bite marks on
them, suggesting these two giants
fight each other. In one case a
T. rex even broke off a *Triceratops*'s
horn. A glimpse of an epic battle like
this would make a great photo.

ST DINOSAURS

AGE OF GIANTS

YOU ARE HERE

END OF THE DINOSAURS

ICE AGE

AGE OF HUMANS

SEE THE DEATH OF THE
DINOSAURS

Devastating collision
You won't want to be anywhere near the meteorite when it hits. Watch from a distance.

If you travel back 65 million years you'll be able to see the global catastrophe that wiped out the dinosaurs. It's an awesome sight. Preceded by a hail of comets, a giant asteroid the size of a city crashes into Earth at great speed, spewing up clouds of dust that block out the Sun to create a cold and dark world. Climate change and air pollution mean that no land animals bigger than a dog survive.

EARLY EARTH

FIRST ANIMALS

AGE OF FISH

AGE OF INSECT

Huge meteorite
The gigantic meteorite that ploughs into Earth is a whopping 10 km (6 miles) wide.

Some **scientists** think that extreme **volcanic activity** in **India** also contributed to the **death** of the **dinosaurs.**

TOURIST TIP

Amazing survivors

"A bit of a surprise!
As we travelled around Earth after the impact we noticed that not everything had died. We saw sharks, crocodiles, birds, and small mammals that had somehow managed to survive."

Activity: Apocalypse tour

CHICXULUB CRATER

The deadly asteroid hits Earth in what is present-day Mexico's Yucatán Peninsula, creating a gigantic crater 180 km (112 miles) wide. If you visit the area a few years after the impact you'll notice that the sea has filled part of the Chicxulub crater with water.

FIRST DINOSAURS

AGE OF GIANTS

YOU ARE HERE

END OF THE DINOSAURS

ICE AGE

AGE OF HUMANS

WHERE TO GO

Visit Europe to see a spectacular frozen landscape and build your own igloo. However, if it's animals that you're after, head to the ice-free plains of North America, Europe, and Asia, just south of the great ice sheets. Here you'll see spectacular herds of grass-eating mammals with their predators – sabre-toothed cats, cave bears, and dire wolves – not far behind.

MASSIVE MAMMALS

Giant sloth
Travel to South America to see a giant sloth, one of the largest mammals of all time. When it stands on its hind legs it's an amazing 6 m (20 ft) tall.

Huge beaver
Try to get a photo of a North American giant beaver. You may think beavers are cute, but this awesome creature is the size of a bear!

Land bridge
North America and Asia are joined by a bridge of land that will disappear when sea levels eventually rise.

Ice sheet
Parts of North America and Europe lie hidden under ice sheets 3 km (2 miles) thick.

ASIA

NORTH AMERICA

ATLANTIC OCEAN

SOUTH AMERICA

Patchy forest
In the dry Ice Age climate, the Amazon rainforest in South America shrinks.

EARLY EARTH

FIRST ANIMALS

AGE OF FISH

AGE OF INSECTS

ICE AGE

PERMISSION GRANTED TO VISIT THE ICE AGE. WARM CLOTHING AND SENSIBLE SHOES ARE ESSENTIAL.

ICE AGE

THE PLEISTOCENE

▶ When: **2.5 million to 10,000 years ago**

The Ice Age is well worth a visit. The dinosaurs may be long gone, but all sorts of weird and wonderful mammals have taken over the world. Journey to the middle of the Ice Age, when the mammals are growing to huge sizes and have thick coats to help keep out the cold. Look out for woolly mammoths and sabre-toothed cats – as well as our early human ancestors.

EUROPE

AFRICA

Arid Africa
Earth's climate is much drier in the Ice Age, and the Sahara desert is larger than it is in modern times.

Mammals haven't just appeared in the Ice Age – they've been around since the **Triassic.** Back then they were **small, furry animals** like mice.

DINO DETECTIVE

Deinotherium's upside-down tusks are a puzzle. They might be used to drag down high branches, but no one is sure. To solve the mystery, visit Ice Age Africa or Asia and look out for this prehistoric cousin of modern elephants.

Growing ocean
The Atlantic Ocean has reached its modern size in the Ice Age.

FIRST DINOSAURS   **AGE OF GIANTS**   **END OF THE DINOSAURS**

YOU ARE HERE

ICE AGE

AGE OF HUMANS

CAGE DIVE WITH A
MEGALODON

For the ultimate prehistoric adventure lower yourself into the sea in a shark-proof cage to see one of the biggest and scariest predators of all time. *Megalodon* is a close relative of the modern great white shark, but it's 20 times heavier and as big as a whale. Colossal jaws and a car-crushing bite make *megalodon* the undisputed king of the ocean.

Dorsal fins
Vertical fins on the shark's back stop it tilting left or right while swimming.

NEED TO KNOW

Size:

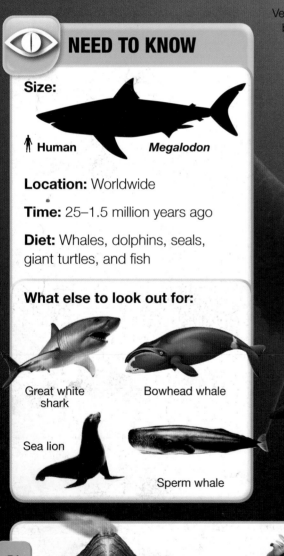

👤 Human   *Megalodon*

Location: Worldwide

Time: 25–1.5 million years ago

Diet: Whales, dolphins, seals, giant turtles, and fish

What else to look out for:

Great white shark

Bowhead whale

Sea lion

Sperm whale

A fully grown *megalodon* can weigh as much as **50 tonnes** – that's the same as **15 adult elephants.**

EARLY EARTH   **FIRST ANIMALS**   **AGE OF FISH**   **AGE OF INSECTS**

Sense of smell
An incredible sense of smell enables *megalodon* to sniff out victims that are too far away to see.

Shark cage
Only a reinforced shark cage can withstand *megalodon*'s bite. Be sure to stay inside the cage during your dive.

Black eye
When *megalodon* lunges to bite, its huge black eyes roll back into the head and give it a white-eyed look.

Meat slicers
The teeth have serrated edges like the cutting edge of a carving knife – perfect for slicing flesh.

TOURIST TIP

Giant tooth

"Terrifying!
By comparing *megalodon*'s teeth to those of a great white shark, you can see exactly how this monster got its scientific name, which means "giant tooth". The teeth can reach 17 cm (7 in) in length.

Attraction: Scuba safari

PHOTO OPPORTUNITY

A shark this large has a very big appetite and often feeds on whales. With a bite five times stronger than that of *T. rex*, it has no problem tearing through the skin and bones of these giant mammals. It's advisable to keep your distance from *megalodon* when it's in hunting mode.

FIRST DINOSAURS

AGE OF GIANTS

END OF THE DINOSAURS

YOU ARE HERE

ICE AGE

AGE OF HUMANS

55

NEED TO KNOW

Size:

Smilodon

Human

Location: North and South America

Time: 2.5 million–10,000 years ago

Diet: Bears, horses, and young mammoths

What else to look out for:

Dire wolf

Titanis

Glyptodon

Pliohippus

Teratornis

Smilodon uses its **immense strength** to overpower prey, before **carving open** the victim's throat with its canine teeth.

Giant teeth
Smilodon's huge canines grow to 25 cm (10 in) long and have a sharp, saw-like edge for slicing flesh.

Warm coat
Smilodon is covered in thick fur to keep it warm in freezing-cold conditions.

SNOWMOBILES

Hop on a snowmobile for the best view of a group of *Smilodons*. Perfect in the snowy conditions, they're also fast enough to escape a sabre-toothed cat if it decides it likes the look of you.

EARLY EARTH

FIRST ANIMALS

AGE OF FISH

AGE OF INSECTS

TRACK A
SMILODON

Muscular body
Stronger and twice the weight of a lion, *Smilodon* is built to bring down huge animals.

Go on an organized safari tour to track down *Smilodon*, a large sabre-toothed cat. An expert ranger will show you how to find their distinctive paw prints in the snow, and these should lead you straight to the fearsome Ice Age predators. *Smilodons* live in big family groups, like modern lions, and can often be found gathered around a kill.

Tiny tail
Unlike lions and tigers, *Smilodon* has a short stub of a tail.

FIRST DINOSAURS

AGE OF GIANTS

END OF THE DINOSAURS

YOU ARE HERE

ICE AGE

AGE OF HUMANS

Hair ....
Brown-red hair
can grow up to
90 cm (3 ft) long.

NEED TO KNOW

Size:

Human

Woolly Mammoth

Location: Europe, North America, Asia

Time: 800,000–4,000 years ago

Diet: Grasses

What else to look out for:

Woolly rhino

Saiga antelope

Neanderthal

Reindeer

EARLY EARTH

FIRST ANIMALS

AGE OF FISH

AGE OF INSECTS

RIDE A WOOLLY MAMMOTH

Journey to the frozen north to ride one of the largest mammals that has ever roamed the planet. Mammoths are almost genetically identical to modern elephants, but they have thick layers of hair to keep them warm in the freezing Ice Age winters. They also have larger curved tusks and much smaller ears.

Tusks
Male mammoths use their long tusks to impress females.

Huge tusks are used like a **plough** to clear away **snow** and **ice** so mammoths can feed on the grasses hidden underneath.

CAVE PAINTING

You won't be the first person to see a mammoth. These huge beasts often come into contact with our early human ancestors, who sometimes set up mammoth traps. In a few years prehistoric people might even hunt mammoths to extinction.

ST DINOSAURS

AGE OF GIANTS

END OF THE DINOSAURS

YOU ARE HERE
ICE AGE

AGE OF HUMANS

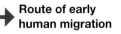
WHERE TO GO

If you want to see the earliest humans travel to Africa. Known as *Homo habilis*, these small and hairy people still look a bit like apes, but instead of spending their time in the trees they walk on the ground using two legs. They're some of the first humans to make tools, which they use for butchering animals they have hunted for food.

TOURIST TIP

Around the campfire

"Hot stuff!
We joined a group of prehistoric people huddled around a campfire in Europe half a million years ago. They are the first people to use fire to cope in the cold conditions. It kept us warm and we were able to cook meat, making it easier to eat."

⭐⭐⭐⭐⭐

Activity: Camping trip

First Europeans
Homo georgicus arrives in Europe 1.7 million years ago.

Neanderthals
Visit Gibraltar 28,000 years ago to meet the last Neanderthals.

EUROPE

AFRICA

First humans
You'll find the earliest humans in East Africa at the start of their journey.

EARLY EARTH

FIRST ANIMALS

AGE OF FISH

AGE OF INSECTS

AGE OF HUMANS

DAWN OF THE MODERN WORLD

> **When: 2 million years ago to present**

If you want to meet a prehistoric human, head to Africa two million years ago to see several species of human living, hunting, and socializing on the dusty plains. This is a defining moment in history. A few brave groups are setting off on an epic journey over deserts, jungles, and mountains that will take them to Europe and Asia for the first time.

ASIA

NDIAN OCEAN

Far East
Humans reach Indonesia 1.8 million years ago.

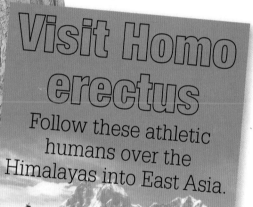

Visit Homo erectus
Follow these athletic humans over the Himalayas into East Asia.

FLINT TOOLS

Some humans have developed stone tools, which they use to kill animals, cut wood, and to defend themselves. Sit down with a family to see how they shape their spear heads, and have a go at making your own.

IRST DINOSAURS

AGE OF GIANTS

END OF THE DINOSAURS

ICE AGE

YOU ARE HERE

AGE OF HUMANS

61

GO CAMPING WITH
NEANDERTHALS

The best way to get to know the Neanderthals, a species of prehistoric human, is to stay with a family. Travel back 28,000 years to Gibraltar, at the bottom of Spain, to meet the last surviving Neanderthals. They're shorter and stronger than modern humans, but share many similarities with us, including the ability to talk and make tools.

NEED TO KNOW

Size:

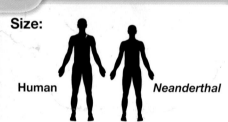

Human   *Neanderthal*

Location: Europe and Asia

Time: 350,000–28,000 years ago

Diet: Deer, boar, grain, marine mammals, and shellfish

What else to look out for:

Wild boar   Ibex

Monk seal

Bottle-nosed dolphin   Red deer

Collecting mussels
Hunting large animals is dangerous, so Neanderthals try to gather food instead.

EARLY EARTH   **FIRST ANIMALS**   **AGE OF FISH**   **AGE OF INSECTS**

Red hair
Many Neanderthals
have pale skin and
reddish-brown hair.

Cave dwellings
Neanderthals shelter in
caves during the chilly
European winters.

💬 TOURIST TIP

Intelligent life

"What clever people!
I was expecting Neanderthals
to be stupid cavemen, but they
aren't at all! They talked with
each other, made us necklaces
out of shells, and even buried
one of their dead.*"*

⭐ ⭐ ⭐ ⭐ ⭐

Activity: Camping trip

Body art
Necklaces, pierced shells,
and body paint are used
by Neanderthals to
decorate their bodies.

The last
Neanderthals
live at the **same**
time as **modern**
humans, but
not for very long.

FIRST DINOSAURS   AGE OF GIANTS   END OF THE DINOSAURS   ICE AGE

YOU ARE HERE

AGE OF HUMANS

INDEX

ACKNOWLEDGMENTS

Dorling Kindersley would like to thank Scarlett O'Hara for proofreading and Chris Bernstein for the index.

The publisher would like to thank the following for their kind permission to reproduce their photographs:

(Key: a-above; b-below/bottom; c-centre; f-far; l-left; r-right; t-top)

6–7 Science Photo Library: Mark Garlick. 6 Dorling Kindersley: Atlantic Digital (fbl); NASA (cl); Andrew Kerr (br). 7 Corbis: Frans Lanting (crb); Roger Ressmeyer (tc). Dorling Kindersley: Centaur Studios – modelmakers (bc); Jon Hughes (bl, br). Science Photo Library: Lynette Cook (cra). 8–9 Science Photo Library: Chris Butler. 8 Dorling Kindersley: Atlantic Digital (fbl); Andrew Kerr (br). 9 Alamy Images: AF archive (crb). Dorling Kindersley: Centaur Studios – modelmakers (bc); Jon Hughes (bl, br). 10 Dorling Kindersley: Atlantic Digital (fbl); Andrew Kerr (br). 11 Corbis: James L. Amos (cb). Dorling Kindersley: Centaur Studios – modelmakers (bc); Rough Guides (crb); Jon Hughes (bl, br). 12 Alamy Images: Amar and Isabelle Guillen – Guillen Photography (tc). Dorling Kindersley: Atlantic Digital (fbl); Andrew Kerr (br). 13 Dorling Kindersley: Centaur Studios – modelmakers (bc); Jon Hughes (bl, br). 14 Dorling Kindersley: Atlantic Digital (fbl); Andrew Kerr (br). 15 Alamy

Images: McPHOTO / vario images GmbH & Co.KG (cra). Dorling Kindersley: Centaur Studios – modelmakers (bc); Jon Hughes (bl, br). 16 Dorling Kindersley: Atlantic Digital (fbl); Andrew Kerr (br). 17 Corbis: Paul Souders (cr, crb). Dorling Kindersley: Centaur Studios – modelmakers (bc); Andrew Kerr (tl, ca); Natural History Museum, London (cra, fcra); Jon Hughes (bl, br). 18 Dorling Kindersley: Atlantic Digital (fbl); Andrew Kerr (br). 19 Alamy Images: Cathy Melloan (bc). Dorling Kindersley: Centaur Studios – modelmakers (bc); Jon Hughes (bl, br). 20–21 The Natural History Museum, London: Graham Cripps. 20 Dorling Kindersley: Atlantic Digital (fbl); Andrew Kerr (br). 21 Dorling Kindersley: Centaur Studios – modelmakers (bc); Jon Hughes (bl, br). 22 Dorling Kindersley: Atlantic Digital (fbl); Jamie Marshall (cla); Andrew Kerr (br). 23 Dorling Kindersley: Centaur Studios – modelmakers (bc); Jon Hughes (bl, br). 24 Dorling Kindersley: Atlantic Digital (fbl); Andrew Kerr (br). 25 Dorling Kindersley: Centaur Studios – modelmakers (bc); Jon Hughes (bl, br). Science Photo Library: Julius T. Csotonyi (crb). 26 Corbis: Andreas Kunert (clb / background). Dorling Kindersley: Atlantic Digital (fbl); Andrew Kerr (br). 27 Dorling Kindersley: Centaur Studios – modelmakers (bc); Jon Hughes (bl, br). 28 Corbis: Theo Allofs (clb). Dorling Kindersley: Atlantic Digital (fbl); Jon Hughes (c, cr); Andrew

Kerr (br). 29 Dorling Kindersley: Centaur Studios – modelmakers (bc); Jon Hughes (bl, br). 30–31 Corbis: Radius Images (b / background). 30 Dorling Kindersley: Atlantic Digital (fbl); Andrew Kerr (fclb, br). 31 Corbis: Stuart O'Sullivan (fcrb). Dorling Kindersley: Centaur Studios – modelmakers (bc); Peter Minister, Digital Sculptor (cra); Jon Hughes (bl, br). 32 Dorling Kindersley: Atlantic Digital (fbl); Natural History Museum, London – modelmaker (clb / diplodocus); Andrew Kerr (br). 33 Dorling Kindersley: Centaur Studios – modelmakers (bc); Jon Hughes (bl, br). 34–35 Dorling Kindersley: Jon Hughes. 34 Dorling Kindersley: Atlantic Digital (fbl); Robert L. Braun – modelmaker (fcl / stegosaurus); Jon Hughes (cb); Andrew Kerr (fcl / pterodactylus; fcl / compsognathus, br). 35 Dorling Kindersley: Centaur Studios – modelmakers (bc); Jon Hughes (bl, br). 36 Dorling Kindersley: Atlantic Digital (fbl); Andrew Kerr (br). 37 Dorling Kindersley: Centaur Studios – modelmakers (bc); Rough Guides (cr); Jon Hughes (bl, br). 38 Dorling Kindersley: Atlantic Digital (fbl); Dennis Wilson – modelmaker (fclb); Andrew Kerr (br). 39 Dorling Kindersley: Centaur Studios – modelmakers (bc); Peter Minister, Digital Sculptor (cl); Jon Hughes (bl, br). 40 Dorling Kindersley: Atlantic Digital (fbl); Andrew Kerr (br). Getty Images: AFP Photo / Fabrice Coffrini (tr). 41 Dorling Kindersley: Centaur Studios – modelmakers (bc); Jon Hughes (bl, br).

Getty Images: AFP Photo / Denis Balibouse / SportsandNews / Helmut Tucek (cl). 42–43 Dorling Kindersley: Frank Denota. 42 Dorling Kindersley: Atlantic Digital (fbl); Jon Hughes (fcla); Andrew Kerr (br). 43 Alamy Images: Clément Philippe / Arterra Picture Library (cr). Dorling Kindersley: Centaur Studios – modelmakers (bc); Jon Hughes (bl, br). 44 Dorling Kindersley: Atlantic Digital (fbl); Jon Hughes (clb); Andrew Kerr (br). Getty Images: Gallo Images / Stuart Fox (tr). 45 Dorling Kindersley: Centaur Studios – modelmakers (bc); Jon Hughes (bl, br). 46 Dorling Kindersley: Atlantic Digital (fbl); Jim Channell (fcla); Jon Hughes (cl); Andrew Kerr (br). 47 Dorling Kindersley: Centaur Studios – modelmakers (bc); Jon Hughes (bl, br). 48–49 Dorling Kindersley: Peter Minister, Digital Sculptor. 48 Dorling Kindersley: Atlantic Digital (fbl); Bedrock Studios (fclb / t-rex); Peter Minister, Digital Sculptor (clb / edmontonia, fclb / pachycephalosaurus); Andrew Kerr (br). 49 Dorling Kindersley: Centaur Studios – modelmakers (bc); Jon Hughes (cra, bl, br). 50–51 Science Photo Library: Mark Garlick. 50 Dorling Kindersley: Atlantic Digital (fbl); Andrew Kerr (br). 51 Dorling Kindersley: Centaur Studios – modelmakers (bc); Jon Hughes (bl, br). Science Photo Library: D. Van Ravenswaay (cr). 52 Corbis: Frans Lanting (cl). Dorling Kindersley: Atlantic Digital (fbl); Jon Hughes (cb); Andrew Kerr (br). 53 Dorling Kindersley: Centaur Studios – modelmakers (bc); Jon Hughes (bl, br). 54 Dorling Kindersley: Atlantic Digital (fbl); Jeremy Hunt – modelmaker (fclb / great white); Martin Camm (clb); Andrew Kerr (br). 55

Corbis: Reinhard Dirscherl / Visuals Unlimited (tr); Jeffrey L. Rotman (cr). Dorling Kindersley: Centaur Studios – modelmakers (bc); Jon Hughes (b Science Photo Library: Jaime Chir (cb). 56 Dorling Kindersley: Atlanti Digital (fbl); Jon Hughes (fcla); Bedrock Studios (fcl / wolf, cl / titanis); Andre Kerr (br). Getty Images: Photodisc Steve Allen (fcr). 57 Dorling Kinders Centaur Studios – modelmakers (bc Jon Hughes (bl, br). 58–59 Science Photo Library: Christian Darkin. 58 Dorling Kindersley: Atlantic Digital Jon Hughes (fcl / rhino); Kenneth Lill antelope, cl / reindeer); Andrew Kerr 59 Corbis: Charles & Josette Lenar (crb). Dorling Kindersley: Centaur Studios – modelmakers (bc); Jon Hu (bl, br). Getty Images: Denny Allen 60 Corbis: Jeff Curtes (b). Dorling Kindersley: Atlantic Digital (fbl); And Kerr (br). 61 Corbis: Carolina Biolog Visuals Unlimited (crb); Michael Runl Robert Harding World Imagery (cb). Dorling Kindersley: Centaur Studio – modelmakers (bc); Jon Hughes (bl 62 Dorling Kindersley: Atlantic Dig (fbl); Cotswold Farm Park, Gloucestershire (fclb / pig); Rollin Ve (clb / ibex); Kenneth Lilly (fclb / seal) Nigel Hicks (clb / deer); Andrew Kerr Getty Images: Photonica / Nick Da (fcr). 63 Dorling Kindersley: Centa Studios – modelmakers (bc); Jon Hu (bl, br).

All other images © Dorling Kindersle For further information see:
www.dkimages.com